Sister in Christ,
I Need You

Sister in Christ, I Need You

An 8-Week Study for Christian Women

SHANA GROOMS

Sister in Christ, I Need You: An 8-Week Study for Christian Women
by Shana Grooms

Unless otherwise noted, all Scripture quotations are taken from the Holman Christian Standard Bible®, Used by Permission HCSB ©1999, 2000, 2002, 2003, 2009 Holman Bible Publishers. Holman Christian Standard Bible®, Holman CBS®, and HCSB® are federally registered trademarks of Holman Bible Publishers.

Scripture quotations noted AMP are taken from the Amplified® Bible (AMP), Copyright © 2015 by The Lockman Foundation. Used by permission.

Scripture quotations noted MSG are taken from The Message. Copyright ©1993, 1994, 1995, 1996, 2000, 2001, 2002. Used by permission of NavPress Publishing Group.

Scripture quotations noted NIV are taken from the Holy Bible, New International Version®, NIV®. Copyright © 1973, 1978, 1984, 2011 by Biblica, Inc.® Used by permission of Zondervan. All rights reserved worldwide. www.zondervan.com The "NIV" and "New International Version" are trademarks registered in the United States Patent and Trademark Office by Biblica, Inc.®

ISBN: 979-8-218-16554-3

Edited by Karen Cain
Cover and interior design by Karisma Design, karisma-design.com.
Photos by Meredith Ward Photography, meredithwardphotography.com.

Published by Shana Grooms.

This book is dedicated to . . .

Nora Renee, my niece,
and
Anna Jo, my "cousin-niece."

May the Light guide your sister-in-Christ relationships as you grow strong and beautiful in your faith. Following Jesus will forever change your sweet lives and affect all the lives you touch. This, my girls, is our legacy.

Love you,
Aunt "Nayna"

Foreword

I am so honored to introduce—or, to many of you, re-introduce—my best friend, Shana Grooms. I've known her as such for more than 30 years. Over this time I've seen her in the role of daughter, wife, mother, educator, musician, author, and speaker to name a few. Above all, she is a child of God, and because of this role, I also know her as a survivor and an encourager. In her two devotionals, *From Pain to Pearls* and *From Pain to Pearls: The Second Strand*, Shana shares her personal testimony of how God cultivates us during challenging times to bring about something beautiful for His glory. And now, in this book, I am thrilled to also introduce Shana as our sister in Christ.

Shana truly is my sister, but I'm so excited that as you read her letters you'll grow in sisterhood with her too—and (by extension) other women who also take this eight-week journey. As with any group of new friends getting to know each other, let me share a few snippets about my friendship with our girl.

Our friendship first started in junior high band. We both played the saxophone and shared a slight intolerance for over-zealous notes from the trumpet section.

We've shared lots of laughs and classic moments—like singing to cassette tapes (what are those?) at the top of our lungs in her first car.

We've had many long conversations about relationships, dreams, concerns, and rationalizations of why it's fine to eat chocolate chip cookie dough (as long as it's after midnight).

I was privileged to stand next to Shana when she married her other best friend, and she did likewise for me. And what a moment when I held my first child while she prayed with my family to welcome him to the world!

At the heart of our many shared experiences, Shana reminds me that at every turn God is there—loving, listening, fulfilling plans. Sometimes these reminders come through her words, but most of the time it's simply that she is there, a remarkable woman God placed in my life. He knew I'd need her and that our friendship would be a source of real joy.

Shana was with me at a pivotal moment in my Christian journey. At 15 years old, I was struggling to take the step of actually giving my life to God and being immersed into His family through baptism. What if I wasn't good enough? What if I made mistakes? Of course, I would never be "good enough," and I would definitely make mistakes. That's the point; Christ covers me. Still, these questions were roadblocks. Then one night during a worship service, there was a time of invitation. I was stranded, knowing it was time to go and choose Christ, and yet my feet were so heavy I couldn't move. Shana was next to me. As the music played, she leaned over and said, "I'll go with you"... and she did. I wasn't alone, and that shattered the heaviness that immobilized me. I confessed my belief and was baptized. Best decision ever!

You might be inclined to say that Shana gave me a nudge. But a nudge implies a gentle push, and a push typically moves something away from you. Shana didn't push; she was with me. This is often what we need, a friend who is simply with us. Someone who doesn't just observe, but joins us. Someone who sees us, hears us, and sometimes just knows. A sister. Sisterhood in Christ is a beautiful reflection of God's presence and unfailing love in our lives. It's a fellowship with other women who, no matter the circumstances, say (just like Shana did), "I'll go with you."

Through her latest project, *Sister in Christ, I Need You*, you will learn the value of sisters. The first time I heard Shana read a few of her letters, I not only felt gratitude for her as my lifelong bestie, pointing me to Christ; but I was sitting among so many other women with a heart for Jesus, and I felt a new appreciation for each of them. Collectively, our sisters are an invaluable resource—with personal insights, encouragement, outpourings of love, and certainly some shared laughs and tears along the way.

My prayer is that this study will highlight the gift of your Christian sisters, while reminding you that you always have a faithful friend in our Father. Through the storms or through the singing, may you hear His voice reminding you, "I'll go with you—and I've sent you sisters who will too!"

LYLAS (Shana can explain),
Jaclyn

Contents

Introduction

For I [Paul] want very much to see you, so I may
impart to you some spiritual gift to strengthen
you, that is, to be mutually encouraged by each
other's faith, both yours and mine.
—————— *Romans 1:11-12* ——————

Dear Sister in Christ,

Paul's desire to be "mutually encouraged by each other's faith"
resonates with me. I love *The Message* version of verse 12 that
reads, "You have as much to give me as I do to you." Wow!

It's a game-changer when we sisters in Christ see equal
value in one another. We can graciously accept that we are all
walking with Christ, relying on His Spirit, and needing His
grace and mercy every day. We can trust that God is teaching
each sister about what He needs her to do in and for His body
(the Church) and that each sister is needed for His purpose.

When we acknowledge that Christ is at work in each of
us, as we are each a part of His body, we understand that our
relationships as sisters in Christ should be sacred. They should
reflect the holy, or sacred, nature of God himself as we follow
God's command to be holy as He is holy (Leviticus 11:44).
When we are living as God's daughters, we take on His righ-
teousness, which translates not only to our own hearts but to
how we open our hearts to others as well. We can view our

1

sisters in Christ as having God's design, His purpose, and His hand upon their lives as well as our own. When we do this, we acknowledge that we are all set apart and all have a part to play in Christ's united body. This can look like a beautiful, yet stark, contrast to the relationships in mainstream culture, which advocates for the pushing of oneself to the front of the line while leaving others behind. God's daughters who are seeking to live a holy life are confident in their "line leader," Jesus Christ, and can, therefore, extend their hands to their sisters and walk right beside them.

Living as sisters in Christ who truly believe that God has planned for us to learn from Him and then from one another changes us from the inside out. We can openly share our needs and our gifts with one another as sisters in Christ. This is why I've written this collection of letters asking for what I desire from you—and I believe the letters not only voice my own needs, but your needs as well. While I have penned the words, they could have come from any of us.

You see, sister in Christ, the longer I journey with Jesus, the more He shows me how much I need Him—and you! This places me in a vulnerable state, but I'm trusting that you will be as careful with my heart as I want to be with yours. I don't know that I could have done this years ago, but I'm opening up to where God is leading me now.

And I'm inviting you, my sister in Christ, to take my hand as we walk with our sweet, sweet Savior. Let's see where He takes us together.

Love in Christ,
Shana

Discussion Questions

1. Who has encouraged your faith the most?
2. Who has God placed in your life to encourage right now in her Christian walk? Discuss specific ways to encourage a sister in Christ.
3. In what ways do you like to receive encouragement? Face-to-face conversations? Text messages? Phone calls? A letter? Feel free to share your own ideas.
4. Why is it important to see equal value in our sisters in Christ? How does this affect our relationships with one another?

Go Deeper

Read 1 Corinthians 12:12-27. Why is it important for sisters in Christ to support each other as a unified body?

Prayer

God, please help me to open my heart to You and to my sisters in Christ as I complete this study.

Live It Out

Send a letter to the person who has encouraged your faith the most.

Reflection

LETTER 1

Sister in Christ, I Need You...
to See Me

That is, we are all in a common relationship
with Jesus Christ.
———— *Galatians 3:28 (MSG)* ————

Dear Sister in Christ,

Have you ever been overlooked or dismissed? I'm sure we all have at one time or another, and no matter the phase of life we are in, it's not a good feeling.

When I was younger, I did not like physical education classes because I seriously did not have one athletic bone in my body (and still do not). Almost every time team captains were selected to choose other teammates, I was chosen after just about everyone else had been claimed. The only way I was ever chosen before the very end was when one of my friends asked the team captain to choose me, basically out of a mixture of kindness and pity.

What I didn't enjoy as a child—and still don't as a middle-aged woman—is being in situations that prompt me to question my worth. I've had to learn that my worth is never going to be determined by someone else or even by me. My worth was determined when Jesus decided I was worth dying for. My worth was established by my Creator when He knit me together in my mother's womb, and He established your worth while doing the same for you.

But sister, the harsh realities of this world can play tricks on my mind, and sometimes I forget that my worth is directly tied to Christ and not to so many other things. My worth is not established by what I do, produce, create, or anything else. And I'm asking that you remind me of this by recognizing and seeing me for who I am: a daughter of the Almighty King and as such, your sister. Please remind me of who I am because of Whose I am.

When you look in my eyes with sincerity because you believe in my worth, it helps me believe in it too. When you treat me as a sister in Christ who does not have to earn this relationship with Jesus or with you, I receive a double blessing. When I'm in a hard season, I need to know that Christ loves me and so do you. Speaking this over me is a welcome song compared to the clanging cymbals of the world that try to distract me from the value Christ places on my life. And if I had to guess, I'd bet that you too have heard the clanging of these same cymbals and would welcome a sweet song.

When you see me, I hope that you can see how excited I am to see you! I love watching you as you walk forward with Christ, seeking Him and His ways. You encourage my own walk by doing so. I look forward to dreaming with you as you pursue God's calling upon your life, and as you carry on, I want to cheer for you and praise God for His leading and your following. When you do the same for me, we are bonded not just for this life but for all eternity.

Sister in Christ, thank you for seeing me. Thank you for reminding me to look to Jesus to see my worth and to catch His reflection in your own eyes as you do the same.

Love in Christ,
Shana

Discussion Questions

1. Has anything made you question your worth or made you feel overlooked or dismissed?
2. Who establishes your worth, sweet sister in Christ? Write your answer here: _____
3. When we base our worth on what we produce or what role we fulfill in other people's lives, how can we end up feeling?
4. What have the clanging cymbals of the world tried to tell you about your worth lately? How does this compare to the sweet song of Christ?

Go Deeper

Read Luke 7:36-50. What does Jesus' encounter with the woman at Simon's house teach you about our value in Christ's eyes?

Prayer

God, thank You for anchoring my worth to You alone. Please allow me to see my sisters in Christ through Your eyes.

Live It Out:

Remind a sister in Christ that you see her this week for who she is: your sister, a daughter of the King.

——Reflection——

Sister in Christ, I Need You...
to Let Me Hear You

But speaking the truth in love, let us grow
in every way into Him who is the head—
Christ. From Him the whole body, fitted and
knit together by every supporting ligament,
promotes the growth of the body for building
up itself in love by the proper working of each
individual part.
———— *Ephesians 4:15-16* ————

Pray hard and long. Pray for your...sisters.
Keep your eyes open. Keep each other's spirits
up so that no one falls behind or drops out.
———— *Ephesians 6:18 (MSG)* ————

Be filled by the Spirit: speaking to one another
in psalms, hymns, and spiritual songs.
———— *Ephesians 5:18-19* ————

Dear Sister in Christ,

Sometimes the last thing I need to hear are the lies that I'm
telling myself, and your voice can help to halt this defeating
process. When I'm fighting the enemy on my own, it's so easy
to fall for his half-truths and lies. But, sister, when I am com-
fortable enough to share with you how I'm really thinking or
feeling, I'm inviting you into my personal narrative.

The lies are always soaked in half-truths when they're from the enemy, which makes them so easy to begin to believe. One half-truth that can be so tempting to believe is that while God loves everyone else, you might be too far gone for Him to love anymore. The truth is, we are all sinners and have fallen short, but God is still right there rooting for us (Romans 3:23). Or perhaps you have been wrestling with the idea that you are not nearly as special as another Christian because she seems to "have it all together." We can neglect to accept that we are all special, yet we all need His grace at work, even through our weaknesses (2 Corinthians 12:9). It's in the middle of this half-truth session within my own mind that I need to hear your voice halt the spiral, reminding me of what God says in His Word.

I'm asking you to step in and speak God's truth over me and into my circumstances. This is the most important thing you could remind me of when I'm trapped by my own insecurities, fears, or challenges. And when you speak that truth in love (as commanded in Ephesians 4:15), a chord is struck, and the beautiful melody plays its way into my logic and my emotions. After all, that's how Christ speaks to us, isn't it?

I also ask that you pray with me, for me, and over me. A written prayer or even a silent one on my behalf is beautiful. When I hear, read, or rest in knowing you are lifting up prayers to our Father, I'm reminded of our relationship as daughters of the King and sisters to one another. I remember that we're not only on the same "team," but we are a part of the same family. There's nothing much sweeter than picturing God's girls coming before their daddy, believing He will help them.

Sister, speaking truth to me straight from God's Word and praying for me is crucial for my growth in Christ. And when I grow in Christ, His entire body becomes more mature. When I pray for you, the result is a stronger you and a stronger body of Christ. It is an honor and a privilege to build one another up in this way!

Encouragers help others stay the course, supporting them as they boldly and confidently allow God to lead them wherever He desires, resting assured in Christ's direction. When your encouragement points directly to Christ every single time, my eyes naturally stay centered on Him. This focus on Christ can change my life, and I will have you to thank for the sweet and genuine reminders.

I'm challenging myself to put this into practice more and more, and I'd like to challenge you to do the same. A strong body of Christ is built when all of us work together.

Love in Christ,
Shana

Discussion Questions:

1. What lies or half-truths have you been prone to believing? Write them down, and then mark them out. Replace each lie by writing God's truth next to it. Utilize His Word, and ask a sister for help if you need it.

2. How do you feel when you know someone is lifting you, or your concern, up in prayer?

3. Who is the best encourager in your life right now? Consider how you could encourage that person this week.

Go Deeper

Read Matthew 6:9-13. What does the Lord's Prayer teach us about bringing our requests before God? How can it help to shape your prayers for your sisters in Christ?

Prayer

God, please help me to bring my sisters in Christ before You in sincere and heartfelt prayer, and to speak Your truth to them in love.

Live It Out

Send a written prayer to another sister in Christ, speaking truth over and into her life.

Reflection

Sister in Christ, I Need You...
to Grow with Me

> You use steel to sharpen steel, and one friend
> sharpens another.
> —————— *Proverbs 27:17 (MSG)* ——————

Dear Sister in Christ,

Growth inspires growth, and more growth leads to even more growth. It's a sort of ripple effect that can impact the body of Christ.

When I see you growing in your authentic relationship with Jesus Christ, I am inspired to grow in my own relationship with Him. When you share what you've been reading, what you've been considering, what you've been wrestling with, or what you've been praying over, I'm reminded that God is the Holy One who cares about having a relationship with each of us.

When we are vulnerable enough with each other to share where we are in the process of growing in a particular area spiritually, we can help each other grow even more. We can do this by accepting where each of us is in the process, because growth happens at different times and rates for everyone, and the growth process is usually difficult. As God prunes areas of our lives in order for more growth to occur, the cutting can hurt. Sharing the raw process of growth with you is a humbling experience that can bring us together in grace and truth. Perhaps God has allowed you to grow in the very area where I'm struggling, and your simple whisper of "God helped me make it, and I know He will help you" is irreplaceable, as it encourages me to keep moving forward.

I understand the power of an encouraging word from another believer, as I have been given this type of encouragement many times. One such time was when I miscarried during 2005, which was my first baby. As I mourned, other sisters in Christ who had gone through this pain came into my living room, hugged me, cried with me, and encouraged me throughout this loss and pain. Knowing that they had taken their same pain to Jesus and seeing that He had carried them through helped me trust that He would do the same for me. Having faithful followers in the flesh who are walking with Jesus empowers us to do so as well.

I realize that if I'm going to be of any help to you in your journey with Christ, then I must make my own spiritual growth a priority as well. Reading God's Word, talking with Him, and always learning more of His ways helps me know how to help you. I must take hold of the opportunity to actively follow Jesus Christ in my day-to-day life so that as our lives intersect, I can help spur you onward.

All growth begins in and continues with, by, and through Jesus. Sister, please point me to Him every single time.

Love in Christ,
Shana

Discussion Questions:

1. What have you been reading, considering, wrestling with, or praying over? Take time to share some of these things with your sisters in Christ.

2. In what area do you feel God is pruning you? Or in what area do you feel God is teaching you? Why do you think this area is important to Him?

3. Fill in the blank with your own personal experience: "God has helped me make it through _____, and I know He will help you." Consider taking turns sharing your sentence with someone. Others may need to know that you have experience around the topic with which they are yearning for help.

4. Create a growth plan for one week, month, or year. How do you plan to grow in your relationship with Christ within your chosen amount of time?

Go Deeper

Read John 15:1-9. Jesus describes himself as the vine and us as the branches. Why is it so important that we stay connected to Him during the often painful process of pruning?

Prayer

God, please help me to grow in my relationship with You.

Live It Out

Meet with a sister in Christ over coffee and share your growth plans. Encourage your fellow sister in Christ along the way and upon reaching her goal.

Reflection

Sister in Christ, I Need You...
to Love Me

> Mostly what God does is love you. Keep
> company with him and learn a life of love.
> Observe how Christ loved us. His love was
> not cautious but extravagant. He didn't love
> in order to get something from us but to give
> everything of himself to us. Love like that.
> ———— *Ephesians 5:2 (MSG)* ————

> Serve one another through love. For the entire
> law is fulfilled in one statement: Love your
> neighbor as yourself.
> ———— *Galatians 5:13-14* ————

Dear Sister in Christ,

Oh, the love of Christ is life-changing! Once we accept His love, He can pour it out through us onto others. Sister in Christ, thank you for loving me so well. I have witnessed so many examples of Christ's love extended to this church body of which we are a part:

I have heard beautiful poetry recited by a dear sister who held a tissue in her precious crumpled hands as she popped her chewing gum.

I have received hugs every Sunday since the day I started attending my church as a first-grade little girl.

I have looked into the eyes of young and old who captivate me with the hope and light that are held in their gazes.

I have tearfully kissed loved ones before they left for eternity and joyfully kissed babies who joined our tribe on this side of eternity.

I have experienced the patience of women teaching me their ways during everyday moments and organized moments, such as in Ladies Circle, allowing me to see what an honor it is to join forces with women serving our King Jesus!

I have listened to words of wisdom passed down to me from women who have "been there, done that" and who have done it so well.

Simply put, I have experienced Christ's love through the Church, and I pray that we as His body continue to show that love to everyone who walks through our doors (and to those who never will). When I gather with other believers, I know that I am with people who are going to love me, want the best for me, and encourage me to walk closely with Christ. These dear people remind me that we are on the same team: His team. My church body prays for my family, including my husband and two teenage sons, and continues to encourage us all to take that next step forward in maturing in Christ. Christ has designed His body to work together, and to properly do so, we must check on one another and encourage one another. And if a misstep is about to occur, it's important to discuss this in love with our sisters in Christ. The love from other Christians is a crucial element of spiritual growth, and I am so very thankful that the Church, Christ's body, continues to help me move forward with Him.

Sisters in Christ, I have needed you and I still do. Let's continue to journey forward together as we continue our legacy of love!

Love in Christ,
Shana

Discussion Questions

1. How have you seen your own church family extend love? Make a list together and record it in the Reflections section.
2. Why is it important for sisters in Christ to establish a legacy of love? How could future generations of Christian sisters be impacted?

Go Deeper

Read 1 Corinthians 13:4-8a. Then read it again, this time aloud, replacing "love" with your name and noting how this makes you feel. In which area of love are you strongest? In which area can you most improve?

Prayer

God, please help others know Your love by receiving my love, which I know is from You.

Live It Out

Choose one way to extend love to your sisters in Christ throughout the next few weeks (or longer).

Reflection

Sister in Christ, I Need You...
to Forgive Me

Above all, have fervent and unfailing love for
one another, because love covers a multitude of
sins [it overlooks unkindness and unselfishly
seeks the best for others].

——————— *1 Peter 4:8 (AMP)* ———————

Dear Sister in Christ,

Because we are called to be in relationships with one another, we will undergo some misunderstandings. This is part of human nature, but we can rest assured that because we are united through Christ by the Holy Spirit, superseding our merely human connection, our relationships can withstand times when we see things differently. When we allow it, Christ can give us peace.

The most humbling forgiveness I've probably ever received was given to me when I didn't even ask. I'm sure that I have offended, reacted unlovingly, responded harshly, or a number of other things without even knowing it—and do you know what my mature sisters in Christ did? They forgave me. They realized that I was not as mature in some areas and that I would learn much more from their love than from their criticism.

I'm not saying that all things should be swept under the rug, but I am suggesting that we take the hurt directly to our

Father—the same Father of the offender—and let Him show us how to handle the misunderstanding, if it needs to be handled at all. If something needs to be discussed, He tells us how to do it: go to your sister alone to explain (Matthew 18:15-17). If this needs to be done, then we must remember to speak the truth in love (Ephesians 4:15).

First Peter 4:8 explains how love covers a multitude of sins. I am used to reading this as a reminder that Love himself covered my sin, but the older I get, I see what else it is saying. It is through love that I am able to overlook unkindness because I truly and deeply care about the sister who may have been unkind in the moment. This is freeing, isn't it? We can trust that God will teach our sisters in Christ, especially those who are not as far along in their spiritual walk, just as He once taught us (and continues to). This is what graceful forgiveness looks like from the sisters who are rooting for you, not against you.

And sister, when we do realize that we have caused hurt, may we run to the one who is hurting and quickly make amends. Christ can help us navigate all things and bring each of us to a place of reconciliation, for we are of ONE body—His.

Love in Christ,
Shana

Discussion Questions

1. Take a moment to consider the times you may have received forgiveness without ever knowing of your offense. How does this gracious gift make you feel?
2. Is there a hurt that you need to take directly to the Father today? Make a commitment to do so in order to be able to move forward.
3. Is there someone from whom you need to ask forgiveness?

Go Deeper

Read Luke 15:11-32. What does the parable of the Lost Son teach you about both seeking and offering forgiveness?

Prayer

God, I thank You for Your forgiveness, and I ask that You help me to extend it, even when my sister doesn't realize her offense.

Live It Out

If you need to seek forgiveness, consider asking for it today. If you are the one who is being asked to forgive, may you seek God and ask Him to help you forgive as He does.

Reflection

LETTER 6

Sister in Christ, I Need You...
to Sit and Stand with Me

Jesus wept.
—————— *John 11:35* ——————

Stoop down and reach out to those who
are oppressed. Share their burdens, and so
complete Christ's law.
—————— *Galatians 6:2 (MSG)* ——————

But those who trust in the Lord will renew their
strength; they will soar on wings like eagles;
they will run and not grow weary; they will
walk and not faint.
—————— *Isaiah 40:31* ——————

Dear Sister in Christ,

As we journey together with Christ and one another, we will
experience various seasons in our lives. I need you by my side
through all of them, whether sorrowful or joyous.

When sisters celebrate joys with one another, the joy
seems to increase immeasurably. When I gave birth to my two
sons, each time I had sisters in Christ come to visit at the
hospital. Could they have waited until I got home? Yes, but
their excitement to greet my little one in this world told me
that they cared for my family and my baby, and they wanted to

37

share in our joy. When sisters are genuinely rejoicing with and for one another, the relationships grow stronger and sturdier with roots connected to Christ himself.

I have also had sisters sit with me during my sorrow of losing my first baby and my last through miscarriage. Two sisters accompanied me to the hospital for surgery, and I woke up to another sister beside me as I lay in bed. I knew they cared, as their very presence showed this. During my second miscarriage, one sister brought food to feed my family, not afraid to enter into my emotionally messy world. We ate, grieved, and talked about how God would continue to walk with me through the pain. A person does not forget these Christ-like examples of love. They will forever be etched upon my heart.

So I ask that when I go through pain or grief, and we know these days will come, please sit down beside me. I might need to just rest my head on your shoulder as we cry together. I may not have anything to say with my words, but your presence is a silent reminder that says, "I'm here for you," and it will be heard pristinely. You will embody what I believe Jesus would do if He were here in physical form, because we saw Him grieve with His own friends. Jesus understands the sorrow of this world all too well, and we can rely on His Spirit to comfort us when grief strikes.

After I experience the grief, my knees may still be wobbly, but when it's time, please stand beside me. There will come a time when I find hope again, but I may need a hand to hold onto as I take this stand and choose to move forward. Your hand may be the stability I need. And seeing that you're willing to stand proves that you, too, have hope in moving forward.

You will remind me that we have Hope and we know Hope—His name is Jesus. He is the one who will beckon us forward to carry on in His story.

Sitting and standing are such simple movements for many of us, but they are so powerful when we do them together. Thank you for your willingness to be there for me, sister in Christ. I promise to do the same for you.

Love in Christ,
Shana

Discussion Questions

1. Is there anyone who needs you to sit with her right now? Has anyone ever done this for you during a sorrowful time? Explain the impact it had on you.
2. Who has helped you stand once again in your life? How did she do this?
3. What does it look like for a sister in Christ to move forward in His hope?

Go Deeper

Read John 11:1-7, 20-44. What do Jesus' responses to His hurting friends teach you about supporting a sister in Christ as she struggles?

Prayer

God, please help me to see when to sit and when to stand with my sisters in Christ and to share with them Your hope.

Live It Out

Silently sit with someone who is grieving, and graciously lend a hand to someone who is ready to stand.

Reflection

Sister in Christ, I Need You...
to Dream with Me

We plan the way we want to live, but only God
makes us able to live it.
——— *Proverbs 16:9 (MSG)* ———

Dear Sister in Christ,

Are you still aware of those dreams nestled down deep in
your heart? You know, the ones you have planted in the soil
of prayer but have not yet seen the bud appear? Or perhaps
you've seen the bud begin to flower, but you don't want to
share because you fear that if the flower dies, you may look
foolish for sharing it in the first place. Sister, I want you to
be able to share those dreams with me whether you are in
the planting, budding, or flourishing phase. Perhaps together,
God will allow us to flesh out what's at the center of that
dream of yours so you can take steps toward accomplishing
it. I'll be rooting for you all along, and even if the flower, or
your dream, seems to wither away, I will be there to remind
you that God's purpose will prevail and that God can still use
broken dreams for His purpose and His glory in His way.

Before I wrote my first devotional book, *From Pain to
Pearls: A 31-Day Devotional for Women*, I shared with a few
sisters in Christ about this dream of mine. I was a bit hesitant

to share because it sounded like a lofty dream that I might not be able to accomplish. However, God put together His story about things He taught me during a time of chronic pain. He crafted the vision and allowed these women, especially my mother, to speak encouragement to me as I laid it all before Him. At just the right time, God made my dream come true. I give God all the glory, and I am so very grateful for my sisters in Christ who prayed me through each step of the way.

While discussing your plans with God is of the utmost importance, as my sister I want you to feel like you can share them with me, and I will commit to praying over these desires with you and for you. If this dream is something God has in store for you, then we know He is in charge. But I'm so honored to be alongside you while we wait for His timing.

I pray God uses us as sisters in Christ who will encourage one another to follow God's lead according to what He plants in our hearts, instead of planting on our own and asking God to water it. Beginning with Jesus is crucial, and I ask that you don't let me miss this. Please encourage me to continue to keep in step with the Holy Spirit as I move forward with Him and as you do the same.

I'm so excited to think of the many dreams that will pass through our hearts during the course of a lifetime. It's inspiring to dream with God and with one another!

Love in Christ,
Shana

Discussion Questions

1. Describe, illustrate, or journal about the dreams you have nestled in your heart. Share them with Jesus.
2. How can sisters in Christ encourage one another as they pursue godly dreams?
3. Map out your first three action steps in order to accomplish one of your dreams. Share these steps with your sisters. Perhaps they can help you check these steps off your list!

Go Deeper

Read Genesis 37:3-20. Joseph had dreams that confused him and angered his brothers, yet God had a purpose for them. What purpose might God have for the dreams He's given you?

Prayer

God, I ask that You plant Your dreams for my life inside my heart and help me water them.

Live It Out

Schedule a dreaming day with a sister in Christ. Create a vision board or verbally share. Pray for each other about these dreams.

Reflection

Sister in Christ, I Need You...
to Be a Safe Place

[Love] bears all things, believes all things,
hopes all things, endures all things.

——————— *1 Corinthians 13:7* ———————

Dear Sister in Christ,

In a dark world, we are called to be different as we believe and follow the Light. Christ, the Light, illuminates everything; therefore, we can always see His hope. But, just in case I decide to keep my eyes closed during a dark season, please lovingly remind me to open them. If what I'm going through seems to have no end in sight, please remind me that Christ has already triumphed and that darkness has been defeated and will end.

I'm asking that you be my safe place where I can express how I'm truly feeling during a difficult time without fear of scaring you away. I need you to love me in a way that bears these things, believes that Christ will see me through, helps me to hope once again, and keeps walking beside me. What a picture of sisterly, Christian love!

Am I asking too much or being needy? The world might say that I am, but Scripture says differently. God says that this is what real love will do, and this is exactly what Love did and continues to do. Yes, it may be difficult at times, but if we are all relying on the Holy Spirit to mold our hearts and lives to be more Christ-like, then I think it's time to claim what true love does—and do it!

When we offer this type of love, we become a safe place for the tattered to harbor, take a rest, and become repaired. It's unique that a person can become a safe place, but Christ has allowed us to understand this concept because that is what He is to each of us.

Sister, I would be honored to be your safe place.

Love in Christ,
Shana

Discussion Questions

1. How would Christ's body be affected if we truly love one another?
2. Are you bearing burdens alone right now? Consider sharing with your sisters so that they can help carry those burdens to Jesus on your behalf.
3. How does the concept of being someone's safe place affect you? Describe what picture comes to mind.

Go Deeper

Read Psalm 23. This psalm paints a beautiful picture of God's love and care for us. What can you learn from this passage that will help you better love and care for your sisters in Christ?

Prayer

God, please help me to love like You do.

Live It Out

Locate an image, or draw one, that represents a safe place. Send that image to someone who encapsulates this image through her presence in your life.

Reflection

Celebration

Encourage one another and build each other
up as you are already doing.
———— *1 Thessalonians 5:11* ————

Dear Sister in Christ,

Now that we have studied God's Word together and have
shared with one another, let's spend our last session celebrating! I've included some ideas of what this could look like, but
feel free to create your own celebration session.

- **Plan a "Sisters in Christ" day out.** Go out to eat at
  a sit-down restaurant with one another. Shop, hike,
  paint, visit the theater—do whatever you want! Just
  soak in a day of relaxation, connection, and fun.
- **Throw a party.** Decorate your classroom or fellowship
  hall, invite each sister in Christ to bring an appetizer
  or dessert, and discuss highlights from the study.
- **Have an evening of encouragement.** Sit in a circle,
  and focus on one sister in Christ at a time as you write
  down (or share aloud) attributes you appreciate about
  her. (Sit in smaller circles if you have a large number.)

- **Treat yourselves to a spa day.** Visit a nail salon, spa, or combination thereof and enjoy! Make sure to take some chocolate along for the day.

Thank you, sister in Christ, for journeying with me under His direction. May we follow Him all our days while helping our sisters do the same.

Love in Christ,
Shana

Discussion Questions

1. What was your favorite part of this study?
2. In what areas can you commit to becoming a better sister to those around you?
3. How important is it to realize the role we all play as sisters in Christ? How could this affect the Church body on a local level and as a whole?

Go Deeper

Read Luke 14:16–23. Who can you invite to come share in the blessings you have received through Christ? Choose a specific person, and pray that God will open doors so that you may introduce her to Jesus and your fellow sisters in Him.

Prayer

God, thank You for Your Word. Please help me to apply it to my relationships with my sisters in Christ as precious members of Your body.

Live It Out

Continue to love and show appreciation for your sisters in Christ well beyond this time of study together. Commit to Christ and to one another as together you journey forward with, and in, Him.

Reflection

www.shanagrooms.com

Made in the USA
Monee, IL
15 May 2025

17517451R00046